SAVING MONEY

A Complete Guide to Money Mastering With More Than 30 Useful Tips for Efficient Family Budget

By CARRIE DRESDEN

Table of Contents

Introduction

If you have never set a budget for your family, you're not alone. A lot of people have never simply sat down to make a budget for the family, but it's something that each family not just needs to do but also something that they have to work out on a monthly basis.

Are you familiar with the saying that goes, "Save for the rainy days"? Of course, you are, but this is a practice that not a lot of people follow. It's true that saving money is the best secret to building wealth. For anyone to meet financial freedom and financial security, having a great amount of saving is important. You're lucky if you were born rich and have a massive inheritance from the wealth of your parents (unless they decided to give it all to charities,) then you are going to be left without anything. Whether you wanted to be rich or not, saving money is important for the benefit of your family. If it is still not clear to you why this should be a part of your family life, then here are 4 important reasons why you have to start doing it now:

#1: It Helps You Survive Financial Emergencies - This is for when an illness, accident, job loss, business failure, or unexpected death affect any family members. These kinds of events have an effect on the family financially. We might find a temporary solution to these problems but this might happen again or it might leave us in huge debt in the end. Having enough savings will set you in peace knowing that you are able to survive any emergency that may happen anytime.

#2: Improve Your Family's Life and Comfort - While some believe that money can't buy you happiness, there is no doubt that it can buy you things that will enrich your family's lifestyle and life in general. Enough savings can help you buy a nice house to live in, a good car to take you anywhere, have a quality education your kids need, or even give you a chance to start a new business. It could also offer simple pleasures like going on a family vacation or even just a simple dinner out. It could also make the married life stronger. A lot of married couples argue about financial matters. With sufficient savings, disagreements about finances could be avoided.

#3: Give Better Life after Retirement - Trusting your future to the government is not enough. The pensions that you'll get from the government and contributions aren't enough to give you and your family a lifetime security. You may end up getting small lump sum amount of money from them after then retirement because of your debts. If this is the case, you may find yourself having to work after the age of 60. What's worse is that you'll have to depend on your kids and it will be harder if they already have their own family. You'll be of less priority in terms of monetary support. So, start saving now while you are younger and able in order for you to enjoy your life after your retirement.

#4: Offers Economic Progress - One of the reasons why you have to save money – patriotic wise – not just for yourself but also for other people is to have sustainable economic progress and financial stability. A lot of first world countries attained the best level of comfort due to money availability from the savings of people in the banks. The money offers financing to companies that are expanding their business that promotes economic development. So, more jobs opportunities are going to be available for everyone. Even small savings can help in micro-financing for small businesses and average people to put up their own business. In a way, the more you save money, the more you're helping your country's economic status.

Chapter 1: 3 Types of Family Budgets

Before knowing different ways and techniques to save money for your family budget, you have to know first the different types of the family budget that you have to cover to master saving money for the family budget. A common misconception is thinking there's just one type of family budget, but the truth is that there are budgets that could help the monthly savings of your family, help your family's financial security, as well as help your family attain its financial objectives.

Type #1: Comprehensive Budget

This type of family budgeting is used for general expenses. This is also known as the Master Budget. This type of budgeting is ideal for families with low income and trying to limit their expenses. This budget includes making lists of your expenses, in a specific category and exact figures broken down by month. It is very useful when you have to reduce the expenses of your family since you have all the details you need to make an organized list.

This type budgeting for the family can also be used in reviewing the money you spent throughout a long period of time, which is basically your overall budget.

Type #2: Problem Solving Budget

This type of family budgeting is for making financial security for a family that is on a tight budget. This is a great tool to work off the family's comprehensive budget if ever there is a problem in keeping the family's spending down in a specific area. Here, making a more detailed list of the area is necessary in order to see precisely where the money is going and to know the things the family has to stop spending on. Basically, this type of budgeting helps the family find the problem on the way they spend their money and get the chance of fixing them.

Type #3: Goal Planning Budget

Now the third type is the type of budgeting that helps the family to achieve their financial goals. This budget works perfectly with the investments of your family. If you're planning your budget for a specific event in your family's life, then this type of budgeting is perfect. It adds more categories to your first family budget for the goal of the family.

In this type of budgeting, you have to first pay for all the family's necessary expenses like bills, rent, groceries, etc. Using the money left, you have to decide how much you want to save up for the goal of the family. In this planning, you don't really have to find out how much money you spend, but how much you have saved.

This type of budgeting is not only very useful for saving for family goals but also for making investments. This column doesn't have to be focused on specific goals, it could also be geared towards savings or emergency funds. Either way, it's an important category to be covered when saving for the budget of the family.

Chapter 2: 30 Tips for Efficient Family Budgeting

Now that you know the importance of saving, learning how to do it would be the next thing you have to learn. Here are 30 useful tips to master family budgeting:

- **<u>PLANNING</u>**

1. Investigate your current spending

The first step to making a family budget is to be aware where the family spends the money. Do you know exactly how much you spend on monthly grocery shopping? Without an accurate knowledge of how much you're currently spending on a monthly basis, it's not possible to plan a family budget.

You can start by gathering all your bank and credit card statements. Every transaction is going to tell you all the purchases you made, when it was made, as well as the total amount. Being knowledgeable about where the family money goes is one of the best tips in budgeting.

2. Collect an Income and Expense Report

The next step is documenting an income and expense report of the family. Don't worry as it is not as complicated as it may sound. This report is just going to summarize for you, at a glance, the income and also what you're spending your money on monthly basis. This report is better to be in spreadsheet format. Remember that it does not have to be fancy as you only need it as your reference. Your family income and spending every month has to be declared on the report in order to precisely define what the family budget needs are.

Take a good look at where your expenses going. This should be everything from the debt to your bills. You should also have to consider the expenses you spend on food together with gasoline and other expenses you can't live without. When you've written everything down you will be able to see how much you really have left over every month after paying for or covering all the expenses.

3. Set or Know Your Goals

Knowing why you would like to budget gives you the motivation to follow it. Maybe you want to free yourself from debt? Or you want to secure your children's education? Or maybe you want to move to a bigger house? Then you'll have to make definite accruals monthly. Know all the things that you want for your family, either they are short term or long term goals. Consider the things that you have to achieve for the next few months or years then continue with your longer term ones. Having goals for your family will help you plan a regular budget to make sure that you achieve them.

4. Make a Plan for Annual, Semi-Annual, or Quarterly Expenses

Most of the time, these are insurance premiums, subscription fees, or gym membership fees that you need to be applied for. When you are trying to save money, avoiding unnecessary payment is important so evaluate these things to see if you really need time. After all, if you are too busy to go to the gym, then just cut your membership and run outside or buy a $100 treadmill or other workout supply that you can use in the long run.

5. Make Everyone Participate

It's not to be considered as a 'family budget' if only one person in the family is doing all the saving. Except you and your husband or wife, the kids must also be a part of this. At the beginning of every month, make them familiar with the money coming in and where you have to spend the income. This is going to make them realize the importance of valuing the money and this would make them more cooperative whenever you tell them that something that they 'want' is out of your budget.

6. Follow Your Plan

Make sure that you follow your budget strictly for at least 3 months straight. This is long enough to see if the plans you made works well for you and each member of the family, and if not, you can make some changes to suit your needs. Make a comparison of your actual expenditure with your budget on a monthly basis to make sure you are not spending too much on a particular area.

7. Expect the Unexpected

Well, yeah, your weekly or monthly expenditures are more insistent and instantaneous than long-term expenditures, but a good budgeting strategy includes both as well as keeps unexpected crises and disasters in mind. Oh, let's also add something that is expected like birthdays, holidays, as well as those one-time expenses.

On the top of keeping the money for special occasions, putting some your income into savings can you see a more precise depiction of your spending money. The entire point of a budgeting is to stop seeing your next paycheck as a lump sum just to provide for occasional occurrences.

- ## <u>SHOPPING</u>

8. Shop for Groceries Wisely

Not just should you eat first before your grocery shopping, try to make it a habit to make a weekly menu and a grocery shopping list in order for you to not end up purchasing things that are not necessary. Also, try to shop for generic products that are cheaper unless it is not smart to compromise their quality. Don't buy anything at the counter table as you don't need most of them most of the time.

9. Choose Quality over Price

Yes, we are talking about saving money, but sometimes, spending more money at a time can save you more in the long run. When you buy something that is worth $50 more than its cheaper alternative, it can be difficult to see how you would be saving money. You have to take your whole purchasing history to prove yourself that you are actually making a saving.

But the point here is that cheaper items tend to break faster compared to quality products. Normally, there is a reason why some brands don't set their price lower.

If you are going to replace your stuff annually, chances are that you are spending more money than you would if you chose to buy the quality product in the beginning.

10. Clip and Use Coupons in Your Purchase

If you add the 5% or 10% discounts that you can save whenever buying something, you'd be pleased to see the amount of money you have saved annually.

Using discount coupons cut out of the local newspaper is also a nice way to save money when shopping at the grocery store. The Sunday newspaper is where most food companies and producers out their weekly discount coupons. Another nice place to search is at the websites of the manufacturer, mainly if you have specific products you're using on a regular basis. What you have to remember about coupons though is to not buy something just because you're going to get a coupon. It is just a waste of money to buy something that you will not use for the sake of a discount.

11. Shop Online

First of all, there are an endless amount of coupon websites online. From the grocery stores, you buy your monthly supply from to your favorite home necessity brands, there are a lot of online coupons that will help you save a lot of money. Websites like www.SmartSource.com, www.CouponMom.com, and even particular grocery stores are offering coupons that you can use online. Online coupons could be a good means to find deals that essentially match the items and brands of your preference, instead of buying random deals from a grocery store around just because you can get ¢50 discount.

Aside from food, there are also some websites that will help you to find ways on how to save money on almost anything you need to buy. Check out the sites like www.Swap.com where you can trade your unused furniture, book, clothes, or anything in your house around your area. This way, you may find something that you may need in your household so you don't have to buy it anymore.

12. Shop for Clothes in Offseason

A good way to save money on clothes is by buying them during offseason. A lot of bigger stores normally display their goods a season before schedule. You will normally find clothes for summer on display during the spring season, clothes for winter during fall, etc. These stores will normally try to unpack unsold items before the selections for the next season arrive, and will normally offer big discounts to move this merchandise. Look for the transition in clothing at the stores, and be prepared to move fast to get the best option.

13. Take Advantage of the Sale

Every one of us knows a person or two who always gets a good deal on buying something. Do you know that you can be this person? You don't have to gain special skills to do this; the truth is they just probably know how to take advantage of a good sale. Yes, most stores put up a big SALE sign on their window but still you find the prices high, well, you should know that 'real' sale can be seasonal.

Always remember that days like Black Friday and Half-Yearly sales that attract the big amount of shoppers for the same reason you have – to save.

14. Buy Secondhand Items

Purchasing secondhand items can certainly require some getting used to, particularly if you are used to buy brand new items. But a lot of stuff can be purchased used in a good as new condition.

For example, it is alright not to buy books from the big box bookstore because you can go to local used book shops and get them for a lot cheaper price. You are not only filling up your kids' bookshelves with educational books, you are also supporting a small local store business. Another thing you can buy as used are toys. Scooters and bicycles are items that most kids want to have and can easily get for discounted amount, but if you want to save even more, then buying second hand is a lot better.

- **LIFESTYLE**

15. Be Healthy Savvy

First of all, you have to be smart about shopping for health insurance for your family. Do not just assume that just because you are paying for a cheap plan, you are saving more money. Assess all the benefits you can get for getting a certain type of health insurance. You may find that a plan that has a higher monthly premium but lower payment for office visits and prescriptions may be your best option.

Also, keep in mind that a lot of drugstores offer free or lower medical care for the entire family. The endless school shots for the children may actually be something you could get at a much cheaper general price at a pharmaceutical office than by visiting your physician and pay a huge fee.

16. Have an Entertainment Allowance

All of us want to be entertained. What is better than looking forward to the weekend because you are going to go to a theater to see a musical play, a concert, or take your kids to the amusement park? We live in a world where entertainment is found at any corner you look at, so let's be real, it is not going to be easy for you to avoid this from time to time.

Many entertainments could be a bit little expensive and most of the time, we don't realize how much going out for a night can break a bank. But by setting aside some money for this specific occasional entertainment, you can make sure that you are not hurting your budget.

17. Do Cheaper Activities

Rather than going to the movie theaters, why don't you just rent some DVDs? Rather than going out to eat on the weekend, why don't you just go to the nearby park or beach to have a picnic or simply have a barbecue party in your backyard? Rather than traveling abroad as an annual tradition, why don't you just go on an exciting road trip and camp out? You don't have to spend a lot of money just to enjoy your family activities. As long as they are fun, exciting, and creative, you will surely have a good time.

18. Avoid Unnecessary Dues like Fines and Penalties

Pay your credit cards on the dot, return videos as soon as you can, follow the law, and so on. The amount of paying for these fines and penalties may seem small at first, but if you just add them up in due course, you'd be staggered to discover how big these fines are essentially costing you.

19. Choose to Drink Tap Water

Drinking water is not just good for the health; it's also a lot cheaper than drinking soft drinks in a can or the coffee that you think you need to get your day started.

About 4,787 bottles could be filled with tap water by only spending $2.10! So whenever you're buying a bottle of water worth $1, you're actually paying 2,279 times of what you would if you filled up the same bottle with tap water.

20. Get Rid Of Vices and Bad Habits

Not just smoking a cigarette can lead to critical medical condition, but its price also grows bigger and bigger, so quitting smoking would be a lot beneficial in many aspects. You could save so much money if you choose to make this decision as well. Just try to calculate of how much you're spending annually for smoking a cigarette, you would feel bad. You could have just invested that money on something more beneficial for you and your family. The same thing goes for drinking alcohol. Of course, this would not be that simple, but if you quit smoking and stop drinking alcohol, you are not only going to save money buying those vices, you will also save money on potential medical bills that could be caused by those bad habits.

21. Ditch on Driving Your Own Car

Ride a bicycle or just go out on your feet. An eco-friendly way to save up on the family budget is to leave the car in the garage and find another cheaper alternative to go around as much as possible. Riding the bike and walking on your feet are good for your wallet as well as your health and the environment.

If you are going further, you can use public transportation. This doesn't only save you money for gas, but as well as for car maintenance, parking fees and a lot more. Every weekday throughout the US, people ride the public transportation 35 million times, so there's no problem if you are going to join them.

Another option is carpooling. You can recruit some coworkers and try to carpool. By driving the average commute of 16 miles per way, you can split the cost of gas with even another passenger and help you save you up to $600 annually.

- **BANKING and SUBSCRIPTION**

22. Use Your Credit Card Wisely

Credit cards are one the main reasons why many Americans are in debt. Having a credit card can make it easier for you to spend more right now and struggle later. Be wise when using your credit card or better yet, just use your debit card or cash. Yes, there is credit card debt consolidation services to help you with your credit card difficulties, but it's best to avoid this problem before it even starts.

23. Take Advantage of the Credit Card for Rewards

If you think using a credit card is more convenient for you than using a debit card or cash, then make sure you use a good credit company. Most credit card providers offer amazing rewards to keep their clients, if your credit card provider is a good company that does this, don't forget to get your reward. Again, just don't forget to pay off your bill every month or you'll end up losing more money in the long run.

24. Know the Services You Don't Use

After reviewing your monthly expenses, your AT&T Bundle invoice might be the first thing you got on your list, or perhaps it is your cable or any television subscription of any sort.

You spend about $10 every month for each premium channel like HBO and Cinemax. Yes, you enjoy watching movies after a long day of hard work, but don't you also pay for the internet which gives you the same service? Dropping off these premium channels will help you save a lot every end of the month.

25. Change your Suppliers

Whether you want to save money on your gas, electricity, phone, or other suppliers, then you can get big savings by 'shopping around.' You might want to stick with your current provider because it is convenient for you, but consider the money you will save up! Visit www.uSwitch.com to compare company prices. There are also companies trying to win the heart of consumers by providing them cheaper alternatives, so take advantage of it!

- ## **HOUSEHOLD**

26. Make Your Own Gifts

Humans are known to be generous by nature and giving present to others on a special occasion is very common. Doing this makes us feel good after all! But even though it makes both the recipient and sender happy, it can affect the sender's budget.

But this shouldn't always be the case. There are cheaper gift alternatives that will still make the person to receive it so happy; one of them is make the gift on your own. When it comes to giving gifts, it is always the thought that counts, your effort on making the gift will be more appreciated. Most of the time, it is better than getting a more expensive gift that wasn't thought about at all.

27. Invest in Re-usable Items

Disposable items are normally cheap and really convenient to use, but not that when you need to buy the items over and over again because you had to throw them away constantly. Your family almost certainly uses a lot of paper products, but why do you choose to spend your money on them when you can buy reusable items?

Paper towels could cost about $1 a roll – instead, purchase a pack of washable cloths also worth the same amount and you will not have to spend money buying paper towels over and over. Instead of purchasing plastic water bottles by the case, you can buy aluminum and filter water bottles for every family member and get it refilled over and over. Before you get a disposable product off store shelves, think twice if there is a recyclable solution instead.

28. Turn Appliances Off When Not in Use

This is no rocket science – you will obviously save a lot when you turn yours appliances of when not using them. Leaving the lights on in your room while you are outside is a big waste because you have to pay for something that you didn't use. The money you can save at the end of the month when you do this may not be that big but when you review the amount that you saved on annually basis, you'll be happy to see the amount that you saved by being practical.

29. Invest in Programmable Thermostat

By using a programmable thermostat you can annually set aside hundreds of dollars on your gas bill. A smart strategy is by keeping your home at a comfortable temperature when you're home and lower the temperature whenever you leave. In the cold season, you may want to set your home temperature at 68°F at night when you're at home and then turn it down to 60°F when you are not at home. With the help of programmable thermostat, you can set the temperature to 68°F one hour before you arrive home. This 8°F is going to add up throughout the cold seasons.

30. Always Consider DIY Projects

So the faucet starts to leak, the drainage clogged, and the bathroom tiles start to form a weird color that is hard to remove. These are things we would normally call someone to help us for. But with little skills and knowledge, this could be done by you.

Before picking up the phone and calling someone for a professional help, you may want to try to fix it yourself. Do-it-yourself repairs have gotten to be totally possible now that demonstrations can be easily watched on YouTube. There are also websites like www.HowStuffWorks.com and www.eHow.com that offer DIY home guides on almost anything. This will not only help you save money but also put out the creativity in you. The Internet is your friend on any DIY projects.

Bonus Tip: Have a Good Attitude and Stay Positive

Keep in mind that when planning for the family budget, there are some compromises that you have to commit to. This includes a lot of sacrifice in order to reduce your expenses and have more money to save up. If you follow it strictly, you will soon start to see the rewards and benefits from these sacrifices. Always stay positive and never get disheartened, life is not easy for a lot of people, but as long as you get your head in the game, everything is possible.

Conclusion

Given the economic state today, people from any state of life can use all the practical tips for saving money mentioned in this book. We will normally think that spending on an expensive item or service is what hurts the budget of your family, but that's not always the case. What people normally take for granted is the everyday expenses that when added up, affect our monthly budget. Getting rid of some unnecessary things and being shrewd consumers will significantly help your family to save a considerable amount at every end of the month.

There are a lot of ways for people to save money on daily expenses. One of the most common mistakes is splurging on groceries thinking that it is for family's well-being anyway. Of course, your family has to eat healthily and follow a proper diet, but these could still be covered even if you become frugal. The key to improving the budget of your family is to consider the future ahead of you. If you have not set goals for where your family financial situation want to be in the next six or twelve months or even more from today, then you have to make a move and do it right now. By doing this, the bottom line is going to improve and your investable level income will cultivate, which in time, going to improve your finances as well as lifestyle.